COMPANION
PLANTING

IN AUSTRALIA

COMPANION
PLANTING
IN AUSTRALIA

Text by Brenda Little • Illustrated by Ken Gilroy

NH
NEW
HOLLAND

Published in Australia by
New Holland Publishers (Australia) Pty Ltd
Sydney • Auckland • London • Cape Town
1/66 Gibbes St Chatswood NSW 2067 Australia
218 Lake Road Northcote Auckland 0627 New Zealand
86 Edgware Road London W2 2EA United Kingdom
80 McKenzie Street Cape Town 8001 South Africa

First published in 1982 by Reed Books
Revised Edition published in 1985
Reprinted in 1986, 1988
In-colour edition published in 1989
Reprinted 1991, 1993 (twice) 1994, 1997
Fourth edition published in 2000 by
New Holland Publishers (Australia) Pty Ltd
Reprinted in 2001, 2002, 2003, 2005, 2007, 2008, 2009, 2010

10 9 8 7 6 5 4 3

National Library of Australia Cataloguing-in-Publication Data:

Little, Brenda
Companion Planting in Australia

ISBN(13) 978-1-86436-627-3

1.Companion Planting
2. Companion crops. I. Gilroy, Ken II. title

635.9

Drawings by Ken Gilroy and Sue Cannon
Cover Design by Peta Nugent
Printed in China through Phoenix Offset

Contents

INTRODUCTION

One of the nicest things about companion planting is the way it puts fun back into gardening. There is naughty pleasure in being able to outwit one's enemies and an enjoyable, cocky sense of one-up-manship when simple measures produce marked results.

Chemical control of a garden calls for retribution for damage done and preventative murder to keep pests and damage down. It can be an expensive business. There are few laughs in it.

A lot of the hints in this book were picked up from my grandfather who was a smiling man and an untidy gardener. When you poked his cabbages they squeaked with health; his beans snapped with a crack like a pistolshot and you needed a bib when you ate one of his apples. 'Nature isn't tidy,' he used to say, loading us up with flowers and veggies all picked from the same patch. You never saw bare soil in his garden. He believed in jostling his plants together and he never used a bought spray in his life. We thought he was a scream. It is only now one realises what a wise old bird he was as more and more people recognise the good sense of working with nature instead of trying to club it into submission.

One is naturally not daft enough to claim that companion planting and the hints given here will give a wholly pest and trouble-free garden but there is very little cost involved and at least you will be doing no harm. I hope you find these reasons cheerful and comfortable enough to make you want to have a go at trying things out.

Brenda Little.

A

Allelopathy

Allelopathy means growth inhibition as the consequence of the influence of one organism on another. You could look the word up and not find it in six dictionaries out of seven.

The experiments necessary to turn it into an exact science have not yet been made, but gardening has been going on for a long time and people aren't stupid. They notice things. They may not know why something happens but they usually register the happening.

When tomatoes and potatoes planted close together have, for three years in a row, produced tomatoes too languid to hold their fruit and potatoes like marbles, but have come up with bumper crops in the fourth year when they were planted at opposite ends of the garden, something clicks. The reason may be obscure but the result is what is important and once you have the proof of the pudding you stick to the recipe.

The information gathered together in this little book is the proof of other people's puddings. For those who pine for scientific reasons as to why plants can make good or bad neighbours, well, it has a lot to do with exhalations, scents and root excretions. Halitosis, body-odour and whiffy socks are no higher in the plant popularity stakes than our own. But there's no accounting for tastes; plants can prefer strange bedfellows. Like us they have their Dr Fells and seemingly irrational love-objects. A delightful American humorist once put her finger right on it. 'Contentment,' she said, 'is a matter of whom's with who'. That's what allelopathy is all about.

Ants

'Go to the ant, thou sluggard; consider her ways and be wise.' The biblical exhortation must have saved the life of many an ant. Not the white ant, of course; everybody knows that destructive habits like that can expect no quarter, not even from the Bible, but those industrious little creatures which show such admirable devotion to duty surely deserve our indulgence, do they not?

No. Not if you do as you are told and consider their ways. Ants protect aphids. They love the 'honey-dew', the sweet substance produced by aphids and go to great lengths to look after their 'milking herds'. They carry aphids from plant to plant and thereby spread virus disease through the garden. They protect other insects whose secretions are tasty but which damage the plants the gardener is attempting to grow. The interests of the ant and the gardener do not coincide.

If you still cannot bring yourself to exterminate these earnest little workers you can at least discourage them. Ants won't go near plants which have bone-meal sprinkled round them. Ants sheer away from plants which are protected by sawn-off, plastic milk-cartons.

Ants hate the scents given off by tansy, pennyroyal and southernwood. A patch of these pleasant, pungent plants by the back door will prevent ants from crossing the threshold. Sprays of these herbs, either fresh or dried, placed on larder shelves will make ants who have got in make a hasty exit.

If you have become exasperated enough to feel murderous, spray the nest with pyrethrum or garlic laced with white pepper. Any nip you may get during the operation can be taken as rough justice exacted for the fact that a good job of aerating the soil was being done before you interfered.

Aphids

Aphids are plant lice and the only good thing to be said about them is that they are easy to see and to destroy.

They can be green, yellow, black or red; they parasite most cultivated plants and become known by the name of the plant they attack — rose aphids, citrus aphids, carrot aphids, strawberry aphids etc. The black variety attack the growing shoots of the broad bean.

Aphids do not like orange-coloured nasturtiums. You may not like them either but if you grow a border of them around a bed of plants you wish to protect you can use the seeds, pickled, instead of capers.

Aphids puncture a plant and suck its sap and while doing so, give off a sticky 'honey-dew' which rapidly becomes mouldy and makes the plant look messy. As explained in the paragraph about ants, 'honey-dew' is an ant delicacy and they will nurse-maid the aphids in

southernwood, penny royal and geranium at the backdoor step will deter ants

11

order to ensure their food supply and, in carrying them from plant to plant, help the spread of virus disease.

The finger and thumb method of killing both aphids and ants is easy but tedious and messy. A strong blast of cold water on aphid-ridden plants will clear a lot of the pests away. A soapy-water spray followed by a rinse with clean water is even better. 'Tea' made from garlic, nettles, basil or wormwood *(see Herb Teas for methods of making)* used as a spray is the best of the lot.

Clumps of those particular herbs grown near plants you wish to protect will make the area less attractive to the aphids.

If you meet a ladybird in the garden coax it to your aphid-ridden plants. It will eat about 400 of the pests in a week.

If driven to buy a commercial spray stick with pyrethrum or nicotine — these sprays kill on contact and do no further harm.

ladybirds eat four hundred aphids in a week

Apples

Apple trees are happier when grass is kept away from their growing area. Grass roots have a breath which shrivels the tender root-tips of the tree.

Clumps of chives grown around apple trees inhibit the formation of apple-scab. If you have apple-scab, spray with a tea made from chives or horse-tail. See Herb Teas.

Foxgloves grown around or beneath apple trees both look pleasant and impart vitality and the strength to resist disease to all plants growing nearby. The keeping quality of apples grown on trees with foxgloves in the vicinity is improved. The foxglove is an extra-ordinary plant *(for more about it see Foxglove)* and it seems unfair that, after all the benefits it gives us the flower should have been chosen to represent the emotion 'insincerity'. The sweet-scented wall-flower and the apple tree do all the better for growing near each other. The potato is much more likely to go down with Phytophtora blight if you plant apples near the potato patch.

The distinctive smell noticed when apples are being stored is from the ethylene gas they give off. Keep carrots and potatoes well away from them or the carrots will turn bitter and the potatoes become tasteless and start to rot.

apple trees are happier when grass is kept away from them

Apricots

The roots of the apricot tree and the roots of the tomato plant don't like each other and are best kept well apart.

Clumps of basil, tansy or southernwood planted around your apricots won't save them from the fruit-fly entirely but their scent is likely to make the pest try somewhere else first.

Assassin bug

Stay your hand if you see an insect that looks like a praying mantis, is brown and has long wings. These bugs eat caterpillars, aphids and leaf-hoppers. They gained their unattractive name from the way they stab their victims and then suck them dry after paralysing them with their toxic saliva. Don't panic if you should happen to get stung; damage will be slight though temporarily painful.

Asters

Pests find the leaves of perennial asters disagreeable to the smell and bitter to the taste, so they are good flowers to grow both for massing and cutting.

Asparagus

Asparagus is said to grow especially well when grown with a mulch of hay and left undisturbed except for picking. A rotting hay mulch still contains a food supply. When you think how animals rely on hay as a foodstuff it is no surprise to find it also good for plants. Asparagus also enjoys the company of tomatoes and parsley.

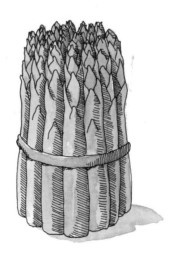

B

Banana skins

The skin of the banana is surprisingly rich in calcium, sodium, silica, sulphur, magnesium and phosphates. Tucked under the top-soil around rose-bushes or geraniums it is one of the simplest and quickest ways of providing valuable plant-food.

you can't have too much basil in a garden

Basil

You can't have too much basil in a garden.

Bush Basil, which only grows to 30 cms in height; Sweet Basil, which grows to three times the size, and Ornamental Basil, which has purple leaves and doesn't look like either of them — all are the gardeners' friend. Bees love basil, aphids, fruit-fly, white-fly and the house-fly hate it.

It can be used as an ornamental border around the tomato patch and the plants will find it easier to resist disease and the fruit will take on added flavour. Nobody would claim basil to be a total deterrent to the fruit-fly, but every little helps and the plants look pretty around your peach and apricot trees.

White-fly won't come near it. Tuck a plant or two near fuchsias and give them protection.

Pots of basil on window-sills, near open doors and outside eating areas will drive the house-fly away.

A sprinkling of the powdered leaves adds zest to sliced tomatoes, salads and soups.

Early botanists warned that those delighted enough by the smell of basil to take the powder of the dry herb and snuff it up the nose would turn mad and die with a nest of scorpions in the brain. Statistics don't seem to prove their findings.

Rue and basil, although they both repel house-flies, do each other nothing but harm. Rue is very bitter and basil is sweet.

Bay

Bay leaves in stored grains such as wheat, rye, beans, oats etc. will repel weevils.

Beans

The bean family, Leguminosae, is large. Here we are only concerned with the broad bean, the French bean and the climbing beans most often found in the family garden.

Beans have the ability to fix nitrogen in the soil. It is necessary to remember this when choosing a crop to sow in the ground they have vacated. Nitrogen encourages leafy growth.

Runner beans are happy to occupy the same space, year after year. Family hair clippings, dog and cat combings, sodden newspapers and the emptyings of the vacuum cleaner put in their trench before planting will make them even happier. They love the mineral and chemical properties in the mixture.

Dwarf beans, beetroot and potatoes planted in alternate rows in their own little patch will help each other to stay healthy and make a

bay leaves will repel weevils in stored grains

good yield. Broad beans and potatoes planted near each other each inhibit the pests which attack the other. All beans grow well near carrots, cucumbers, cabbage, lettuce, peas, parsley and cauliflower. All beans grow badly if near onions, garlic, fennel or gladioli.

It's easy to understand why they might not like the first three but what can be repellent about the beautiful gladioli? Something obviously is, for beans are not the only plants to dislike them.

Climbing beans should not be planted near sunflowers as they fight each other for light and space.

Broad beans grow better if planted in alternate rows with spinach which shades the soil and keeps it damp.

Beer

There is nourishment in beer. The rinsings of empty beer bottles will be appreciated by indoor plants, plants in tubs and border flowers.

Bees

Bees do a good job of plant pollination so it makes good sense to attract them to the garden. They love lavender, fennel, lemon balm, basil, coriander, thyme, borage.

Beetles

Many people kill beetles on sight. Some black and brown shield-shaped beetles have the sense to keep out of the way during the day and come out at night to feed on snails and caterpillars. If one has got his timing wrong, give him a chance to get back into hiding.

Beetroot

Beetroot grows well with onions, silver beet, kohlrabi, lettuce, cabbage and dwarf beans.

It does not grow well near tall beans. This could be because the beans don't allow it enough light.

Birds

Birds are the gardener's ally quite as often as they are his enemy. They rely on insects for up to 50% of their diet and will feed on them in preference to anything else. Silver-eyes love aphids and caterpillars, yellow robins and thrushes love caterpillars and moths and will be attracted to a garden which has banksias, melaleucas, grevilleas, bottle-brushes and hakeas growing there.

You will have to watch it though with currawongs and kookaburras. They kill smaller birds, lizards, and the worms the

kookaburras kill smaller birds, lizards, and the worms the gardener needs gardener needs. Sparrows and cockatoos can be nothing but a nuisance as they tend to get to the ripening harvest first.

With regard to birds the gardener will often find himself in a quandary. Each one will have to make a decision as to whether to encourage these beautiful creatures.

Borage

Borage is said to be the herb of courage. It is a pretty thing with blue flowers and leaves which taste of cucumber. Strawberries grown near it certainly take heart and fight off disease and produce bigger and better-tasting fruit.

Broccoli

Broccoli belongs to the cabbage family and has the same characteristics, one of which is the ability to stunt the growth of strawberries. (*See cabbage.*)

Brussels sprouts

Brussels sprouts don't do strawberries any good either. Their own troubles mostly come from attack by mildew and the cut-worm.

A light spray of seaweed (see p.74) will help them to combat mildew and narrow collars of tarred paper, or even of plain cardboard will deter the cut-worm. The collars are very easy to make.

Cut the paper of cardboard into 7 centimetre widths. Cut off in lengths sufficient to make a neat circle around the plant and staple together. Drop over the plant, sinking a few centimetres of the collar beneath the soil.

Butterflies

Butterflies can be a problem in that most of them are harmless to plants and may even aid their pollination, but their young are a different matter. Caterpillars eat the leaves, shoots, flowers and roots of plants the gardener is trying to grow. The pleasure of seeing the beautiful gauzy-winged parents hovering above the flowers will have to be paid for later.

C
Cabbages

Cabbages grow well in the company of beans and beetroot, celery, mint, thyme, sage, rosemary and dill, onions and potatoes.

Cabbages do *not* grow well near strawberries or tomatoes. The strawberries and tomatoes don't flourish either.

Don't grow cabbages in the same spot two years running. They will be twice as susceptible to club-root the second year.

Don't grow the herb rue anywhere near cabbages; they hate the bitter exhalation from its leaves and the excretions given off by its roots.

The cabbage white butterfly looks pretty as it flickers over the garden; the trick is to dissuade it from settling on your cabbages and laying its eggs on them. It does not like the scents from sage, rosemary, hyssop, thyme, dill, southernwood, mint and chamomile. A border of one of these herbs will help to keep it away; a mixed border will do even better.

Aphids don't like orange-coloured nasturtiums which can look very attractive grown between and around cabbage plants.

Aphids *do* like yellow nasturtiums. For some mysterious reason they find the colour yellow pleasing and will congregate on the plants. If you grow a few nearby they will act as a lure and give you the chance to eliminate the pests in large numbers.

Tansy will repel both the cabbage-worm and the cut-worm.

Short sticks of rhubarb buried here and there throughout the cabbage patch will help to protect the plants against club-root.

21

Strips of tarred twine or underfelt stretched between the rows, and twists of tin-foil around the cabbage roots will inhibit the growth of cabbage-fly larvae.

Few insects like blood and bone. A scattering over the plants and between the rows will send them elsewhere.

If cabbages show signs of mildew a light spray with seaweed (see p.74) will help.

Camellias

Camellias like tea-leaves.

If you use tea-bags you can slit them, drop them into a container of water kept at the ready and when the colour of the water is a pleasant brown, tip the lot around the roots of the trees.

Carrots

Carrots grow well with peas, radishes, lettuce, chives, sage, onions and leeks

Carrots and onions planted in alternate rows are good allies. The carrots drive off the onion fly and the onions drive off the carrot fly.

Carrot roots give off a breath of something which peas appreciate. When planted together, keep carrots on the sunny side.

The carrot-fly maggots which attack the roots of the plant don't like strong smells. Moth balls crumbled into the soil around the growing carrots, and pungent herbs like sage, rosemary and wormwood planted nearby will keep them away, as will tarred or creosoted string strung between the rows.

When sowing carrot seed try and keep it evenly and thinly dispersed. The disturbance of thinning encourages the carrot-fly.

For a mixed planting try sowing leeks and carrots in the same row. Use slightly more carrot seed than leek seed. The carrots will be ready to harvest before the leeks, which will have acted as protection against the carrot-fly.

Carnations

Carnations planted in soil where hyacinth bulbs have been growing will be poisoned. Carnations get their own back. Hyacinths planted in soil where carnations have been growing will die.

Caterpillars

Pepper sprinkled on dew-wet leaves will protect them from the predation of caterpillars.

Infestations of caterpillars can be killed off by spraying with garlic tea (see Herb Teas) laced with pepper.

cabbage, onions and carrots

Cauliflowers

Cauliflowers grow well near celery which keeps away the white cabbage butterfly.

Cauliflowers and strawberries are bad for each other.

A sprinkling of wood-ash around cauliflower plants will protect them against insect attack.

Cardboard collars fitted around the plant and sunk a little way into the soil will ward off cut-worms.

Celery

Celery grows well near tomatoes, dill, beans, leeks and cabbage. It is particularly happy grown in alternate rows with leeks. They both like compost which has some pig manure in it.

Celery is of benefit to all members of the cabbage family as the white cabbage butterfly does not like its scent.

Centipedes

Centipedes, which are ginger-coloured and have one pair of legs to every body segment, are useful because they live on decaying garden stuff, not growing matter.

Chamomile

Anthemis nobilis, to use its botanical name, is a pleasure to grow if only for the profusion of golden flowers and elegant feathery leaves. Other plants enjoy its company. Mint becomes tastier when grown near it and ailing plants revive. Cabbages do all the better for growing near it. Onions like it — provided it keeps about a metre away.

Chamomile has been called the 'plant doctor' because of its ability to encourage other plants to increase their essential oil and so taste and smell more strongly.

chamomile 'the plant doctor'

At one time an anthemis lawn was popular, not only because insects won't breed in it, but also because it stays green throughout the driest weather and gives off its clean scent when walked upon. But it flowers all the time and can grow tall and lanky and so takes a fair amount of work to keep in trim. Now any chamomile lawn you come across is likely to be the Treneague strain, which never flowers and never requires to be cut. The two strains should not be mixed.

If you collect and dry the golden flowers they can be used to make chamomile tea by soaking a handful in cold water for a day or two. Any young plant which looks sickly will be helped by a gentle dose of the 'medicine'.

Old plants can be grubbed out, chopped up and added to the compost bin to help to activate the composting process.

Chervil

Most herbs are happier grown in company with others. Chervil, which is such a pleasant flavouring for baby carrots, is happiest alongside dill and coriander.

Chives

Chives are almost never attacked by either disease or insects.

Chives and parsley grow well together.

Clumps of chives growing near apple trees will help to keep them free from apple-scab.

Apple trees suffering from scab can be doctored by spraying with a tea made by infusing dried chives in boiling water, letting the water cool and then using at half-strength.

Chives tea is also a useful spray when gooseberry bushes start to show mildew.

Citrus

When planting several citrus trees put in a guava nearby. It will protect them against infections. It is said that a few zinc-coated nails gently hammered into a citrus-tree trunk will ensure a good crop.

Comfrey

Comfrey is a splendid plant to have in the garden. Nothing can equal the comfort of a poultice of its large, hairy leaves around a sprained ankle. The ancients called it 'Knitbone' and they knew what they were talking about.

The plant is rich in potassium, nitrogen and phosphates and so makes a good fertiliser if you soak a handful of the leaves in water for a month and then strain and use as you would any liquid fertiliser. The sludgy mess left is useful too. Tip it around your tomatoes or potatoes.

Comfrey also supplies vitamin B12 and calcium so try it as a refreshing drink made by pouring ¾ litre boiling water over 6 cut-up and washed leaves. Allow it to brew like ordinary tea and then serve with a slice of lemon and honey to taste.

Compost

Making compost is one of the joys of gardening. To find kitchen waste, old newspapers, grass clippings, garden cuttings, vacuum cleaner fluff etc. transformed into crumbly black soil is enormously satisfying. When dubious about putting something into the compost bin just ask yourself if it's ever been alive — if it has, it's OK to put in.

You can buy compost bins or make your own. In each case the bottom layer you put in must be on the earth.

If you don't want to buy or to construct you can at least pile all your waste in a hidden corner of the garden observing the rule of a thinnish layer of waste alternating with a scattering of earth, an occasional scattering of lime and of fertiliser. A properly constructed compost heap is, of course, more sanitary and results are more quickly achieved. The results will probably convince you that it's worth taking more trouble next time.

Most gardening books give a blow by blow description of how to construct your own compost pile. I swear by the bought plastic bins and even more by compost which acts as a life-infusion to the garden.

Coriander

A tall annual herb which looks a bit like parsley and attracts bees. It grows well with dill, chervil and anise but will wilt if fennel is allowed nearby and will, in return, prevent fennel from forming seed.

Dill, chervil and coriander growing between rows of carrots and cabbage will protect them from predation by pests.

Coreopsis

If you want a trouble-free flower which provides lovely blooms for cutting, go for the coreopsis. It is heat-resistant, grows equally well in damp, dry, sandy or heavy soils and seeds easily. Seed scattered in neglected garden spots in autumn will provide a lovely spring and summer show.

Cosmos

Cosmos, like the coreopsis, is unlikely to be troubled by either pests or disease and is just as good-tempered. It will grow in any type of soil and needs no special care except for an occasional stake for support which will be easily hidden in a group planting. This tall, autumn-flowering annual is great for hiding fences.

Crop rotation

It is a mistake to grow the same plant family in the same spot year after year. Continuous demand for the same type of nutriment will eventually render the soil too impoverished to be of use.

An ideal arrangement is:
   a. Fertilise the soil with manured compost.
   b. Plant in it heavy feeders, such as cabbage, cauliflowers, celery, leeks, sweet corn, squash, cucumbers, spinach, lettuce and endive.

c. The following year use the space for beans or peas. The legume family put nitrogen back into the soil.
d. The third year plant light feeders, such as carrots, beetroot, radishes, parsnips or turnips where the legumes have been.
e. Start the process over again.

Cucumbers

Cucumbers are friendly plants. They get on with potatoes, beans, celery, lettuce, sweet corn and savoy cabbages. They love to have sunflowers towering over them and giving them shade. They appreciate the proximity of radishes which repel the cucumber beetle.

If they become afflicted by eel-worm, give them a spray of sugar solution (1 kilogram of sugar to half a bucket of water).

If they become mildewed spray them with nettle tea. *(See Herb Teas.)* Spray them with nettle tea even if they haven't got mildew. It will help them not to get it at all, as well as acting as a fertiliser.

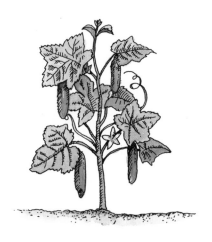

Cutworms

Cutworms have smooth, fleshy bodies and can be any colour from cream through green and grey to black. They feed on the stems of young plants, eating right through them so that they collapse. They are fond of young flower seedlings, cabbage, cauliflower, beans and sweet corn. Tansy is a good deterrent. If you have no tansy growing where cutworms are active, bruise a few shoots and leaves of the plant and strew it around the area or squeeze tansy juice on to your fingers and gently smear it on the stems of the young plants you wish to protect.

D

Damsel-fly

.This insect, which can be distinguished from the dragon-fly by the way the wings are folded down when the body is at rest, is equipped,

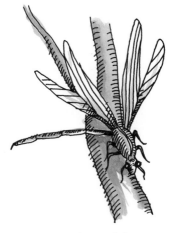

damsel-fly

like the praying mantis and the assassin bug, with forelegs which are ideal for catching aphids and disposing of insect larvae. Leave it be.

Dandelions

Some people use the shaggy, golden heads of the dandelion to make wine; others use the strong, bitter leaves, shredded, to give sharpness to salads, and yet others roast the roots, grind them and use the powder instead of coffee. All such personal experiments have ended in failure. But the dandelion is such a vibrant plant, so rich in copper and bursting with therapeutic qualities that one can only feel guilt in grubbing it up and throwing it away.

It gives off an ethylene gas which induces plants growing in its vicinity to mature early — and this is fine, as far as it goes. Plants spurred on in this way don't do much good afterwards. When the dandelion has grown and produced its first flowers, cut off stems, leaves and flowers and add them to the compost where they can be used to help the mixture mature. The root left below the ground will push up more growth which can be used in the same way later.

Derris dust

Derris dust, made from the powdered roots of *derris eliptica*, is one of the aids which gardeners, loath to use chemicals, feel that they can, in all conscience use. Harmless though it is to plants, animals and humans, it will kill goldfish.

Dill

Dill has been grown since time immemorial. It was known both to the ancient Egyptians and the early Norsemen. Its name comes from the old Norse word 'dilla' which means to soothe. It grows well with

dandelions — rich in copper

fennel and coriander and is pleasant to have in the garden if only for
the reminder it gives of the centuries long chain of fretful children who
slept more easily because their wind was settled by a dose of dill-
water.

Carrots and tomatoes benefit from having it close by as it lures
away pests but it should be pulled before it flowers, for after that it
seems to be of no further benefit to the plants.

Dill attracts bees and repels the white cabbage moth.

A few sprigs of dill added to cooking cabbage will nullify the smell
for which cabbage has such a bad reputation.

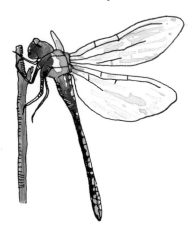

dragonflies — a nuisance to the gardener they certainly are not

Dragonflies

Dragonflies are so beautiful it is hard to imagine that anyone would be
willing to kill them. If you see any about, don't spray. They will be
seizing and killing other flying insects which could be the nuisance to the
gardener they certainly are not.

E
Earwigs

Earwigs look like beetles but can be distinguished from them by their long narrow body and the pincers at the posterior end of their abdomen. They will not creep into your ear but they will come out at night and make a mess of your plants.

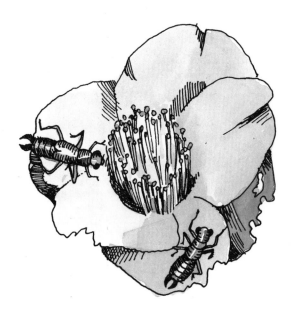

earwigs come out at night and make a mess of your plants

An old perished garden hose can be put to good use for trapping earwigs. Cut into small pieces and scattered around the garden plots it will provide an attractive shelter for these pests which can then be collected and disposed of. Hollow bamboo stems will do just as well. Even an old duster left out overnight has collected them up for despatch the following morning.

Eelworms

These microscopic pests attack both the roots and stems of plants and weaken them badly. They don't like marigolds. A lot of other pests don't like them either which makes marigolds a must for using as a border around vegetable gardens.

If you think eelworms (which are also called nematodes) have been attacking above ground, boil a cup of sugar in water to cover, dilute it, and spray the plants you wish to protect.

F
Fennel

If you have a dog you need fennel in the garden.

You need it as a plant in a pot outside the kennel and for sprays to put inside the kennel to deter fleas.

if you have a dog you need fennel

Pick fennel, scrunch it in your hand until the juices flow and rub into your dog's coat. The dog won't mind. It likes the aniseed flavour — the fleas will hate it.

If you plant fennel in the garden keep it away from all beans, tomatoes, kohlrabi and the herb, coriander. Coriander and fennel have a mutually destroying effect. Never plant wormwood near fennel, as this will stunt its growth or even kill it.

Fertilisers

Rinsed-out milk cartons, beer bottles, tea-pots and any vegetable water you may have are all valuable. Pot-plants grown on window-sills are grateful for such small mercies.

Fleas

Fennel. Fennel and yet again, fennel.

Flies

Pots of basil, tansy or eau-de-cologne mint, or all three, placed in strategic positions will keep the house-fly away from the house and are useful in barbecue areas.

Foxgloves

The old-fashioned purple foxglove is good to grow near potatoes, tomatoes and apples to stimulate their growth and protect them against fungus disease. Foxglove, from which the heart medicine digitalis is made, has the ability to give strength and longer life to plants growing near it. Foxglove tea, made by steeping flowers, leaves and stems in water, can be added to the water of vase-flowers and will keep them healthier for longer.

Frogs

A pond in the garden will attract frogs. Though they may keep you awake at night by their croaking they will also be doing a good job for you. They eat many garden pests, particularly egg-laying adults who could prove much more of a nuisance than the frogs.

Fruit fly

This is a dreadful pest. Plants of tansy, basil and southernwood planted around peach and apricot trees, and any others subject to their depredations, will be helped but it's no use pretending they will be enough to keep the fruit safe.

frogs eat many garden pests

Fuchsias

Once you have ferns in the garden it is unlikely to be long before you find you have too many. Cull the plants, chop the cullings and dig them in round your fuchsias.

G

Garlic

Garlic is something the garden cannot afford to be without providing you remember that peas, beans, cabbage and strawberries don't like it anywhere near them.

Clumps of garlic have been planted in rose gardens for a long time now and there is general acceptance that the pungent breath of the garlic helps to keep the beautiful bushes free from aphids.

Garlic is equally good planted beneath apple trees to protect them against apple scab and under peach trees to protect them against leaf-curl and near tomatoes to protect them against red spider.

Mosquitoes keep away from areas where garlic is growing. Garlic grown in pots and shifted around as need be can be very useful.

Ants, spiders, caterpillars, the cabbage worm and the tomato worm can be killed off by a spray made from 4 crushed cloves of garlic soaked in a litre of water for several days.

A more potent spray is made by grinding up 2 cloves of garlic and 6 hot red peppers and adding them to 2 litres of water made frothy by 2 tablespoons of soap — not detergent. Use the water hot to make the mix and use your discretion in choosing the temperature at which to spray. Plants can be surprisingly tolerant of the temperature at which sprays are used, but test carefully.

Gecko

You are lucky if you have a gecko in the garden. These beautiful little nocturnal lizards hide during the day and come out at night to feed on insects. If you turn over loose bark and find him, let him rest.

garlic

Geraniums

Geraniums are showy plants which add colour to the garden. If you have a grape-vine strike some geranium cuttings around it and the growing plants will repel the Japanese beetle which can be such a nuisance to vines.

Gladioli

Keep them well away from strawberries, peas and beans. I can't find out why they are so bad for these plants and can only say they just are.

Grape-vines

The word goes that grape-vines grow better for being near mulberry trees and being allowed to twine their way among the branches. I've never had the nerve to do this, having enough trouble in trying to collect the mulberries from the tall, madly spreading tree to want to have to clamber after inaccessible grapes but the tip could be worthwhile. If your nerve fails too plant hyssop and basil near the vines instead.

horse-radish

H
Herbs

Herbs are happiest when growing in the company of others so, for culinary use, it is good to have a mixed herb patch.

When planting herbs as protection it follows that one or two species planted together will do a better job.

Annual herbs shouldn't be planted in the same spot two years in succession for they will have taken too much of what they wanted out of the soil in the first year for there to be enough to sustain another crop in the second.

Dried herbs mixed with seed when planting will help to keep away birds, mice and slugs.

Herb Teas

A good general recipe for the preparation of herb 'teas' for spraying purposes is to cover the selected amount of herbs with water, bring it to the boil, hold it for a minute or two, then take away from the heat and strain the water off. Dilute the tea with 4 times the amount of water and use at once. The sludgy mess left can be added to the compost. The younger leaves of a plant are the best ones to use. Once a plant has blossomed the leaves have lost strength. Some herbs require a different treatment and the recipes will be found under their individual heading.

Horse-radish

A plant or two of horse-radish will protect fruit trees and potatoes

herbal tea

against fungus. A plant at each end of the potato plot will be enough and an occasional one will do good in the orchard. When you think of how too much horse-radish sauce can bring tears to the eyes it is easy to understand why pests steer clear. Young horse-radish leaves made into a tea as per the recipe under Herb Teas is useful as a spray when fruit trees show signs of monilia.

Horsetail

The weed 'equisetum' has long been used by herbalists for the treatment of kidney complaints and is versatile enough to have been used as a brass polish. It is a rich source of silica and, when made into a spray is useful against mildew and fungus and, used lightly over young plants, will prevent them 'damping off'. You can buy the dried herb in health food shops.

To make a herb 'tea' boil a tablespoonful of the dried herb in 2 litres of water for 20 minutes. Let the liquid stand, covered, for 2 days, and then strain and use.

Hyssop

Bees love the minty flavoured leaves and blue flowers of this herb, but radishes won't grow well in its vicinity.

Grape-vines do better with hyssop growing near them.

A border of hyssop around the cabbage bed will lure the cabbage moth away from the cabbages.

A tea of hyssop leaves makes a good spray to use when bacterial diseases are present.

Hoverflies

The insect looks like a little wasp but is silent as it hovers above plants and should not be discouraged as members of the family eat aphids and their larvae, mealy-bugs and grasshoppers.

kohlrabi, a relative of the cabbage and the turnip

K
Kohlrabi

This nice little vegetable, a relative of both the cabbage and the turnip, is not grown as often as it deserves, largely because people complain that it is 'woody'. It only grows 'woody' with age and should be eaten when small. It is good grown near beetroot and onions, but must be kept away from tomatoes, which it harms, and beans, which harm it.

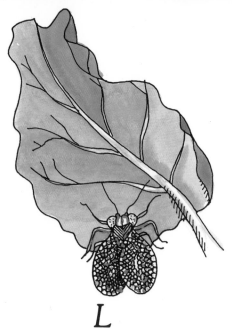

L

Lacewings

These small green insects with four gauzy wings and golden eyes are often seen at night fluttering round an outside light. Their larvae are called 'aphid-lions' because of their voracious appetite for the pests. Lacewings lay their eggs on the top-side of leaves and can easily be recognised by the thread-like stalk by which they are attached to the leaf. If you leave them be the eggs will hatch, and the larvae, equipped with magnificent jaws, will run down the thread, immediately on the attack for their first meal. They suck the body juices of the aphids and then use the empty skins to camouflage themselves. They also eat moth eggs, caterpillars, mealy bugs, scale insects and thrips.

Ladybirds

'Ladybird, ladybird fly away home,
Your house is on fire and your children all gone.'

I can't imagine how the nursery rhyme originated for even in early times the ladybird was a welcome visitor. Their name is a corruption of 'Our Lady's bird', a name given by grateful peasants when a sudden swarm of one of the species arrived providentially and cleared up an infestation of pests which were devastating the vineyards. Ladybirds get through an incredible number of aphids in a week but also enjoy scale insects, mealy bugs, leaf-hoppers, whiteflies, mites, the potato beetle and the bean beetle. They penetrate among plants to places inaccessible to spray, and are the gardener's most useful insect friend. Most people can recognise them in their adult form of red, yellow or orange coat with black spots or stripes but the small spiky torpedo-shaped larvae are often mistaken for pests themselves when they are actually attacking pests.

Larkspur

The larkspur is not fond of heat but, if you can grow it, the blue, pink and rose-coloured blooms both look attractive in the garden and make excellent cut flowers. An added bonus is that their leaves are poisonous to most insect pests.

Lavender

Lavender attracts bees and is a general benefit to the garden. A bowl of dried lavender in a room gives a clean background fragrance and moths hate it, hence the popularity of the lavender bag for use in wardrobes and among clothes stored in drawers. Someone said a bunch of lavender hung in the food cupboard keeps away the moths which accompany stored rice and flour but I don't know if I'd care to have its scent so close to food, although gourmet cooks are using it.

Leeks

Leeks and carrots grown in alternate rows will give each other protection from insect attack. Leeks and celery, grown in alternate rows in ground enriched with pig-manure compost, will both benefit from the potassium supplied. For 'pig' also read 'goat'.

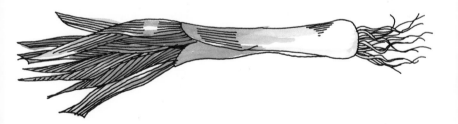

Leaves

The fallen leaf can be the gardener's bane or blessing according to an attitude of mind. Wise gardeners lust after them and, without any of their own, will travel in pursuit of the free bounty. Layers of leaves are a must for the compost bin but should you be considering using them as a mulch, they are best shredded. A layer of solid leaves can make it

lavender attracts bees

tough going for plants trying to push their way to the light. There are machines which render all manner of compost small enough to be more quickly acceptable but, if like most of us you don't have one, but want to use leaves as mulch, run the garden mower over them, backwards and forwards, until they are of a consistency fine enough to be run through the spread fingers.

Legumes

Almost all plants in the garden are helped by association with the family Leguminosae, which, among others, includes the bean and the pea. Legumes take nitrogen from the air and pass it to their roots, which develop nodules which release nitrogen into the soil. Nitrogen produces leafy growth so it is easy to understand why the onion family and the legume family are at cross purposes. But the potato thrives on the nitrogen supplied by pea roots. As a rule of thumb it is simplest to accept that all members of the onion family are at war with all members of the Leguminosae family and that peas and beans come off worst if battle is joined. Fruit trees and grape-vines appreciate finding nitrogen in the soil so they can be planted, with advantage, where peas and beans have been growing and will appreciate their continued close companionship.

Lemon balm

This is a dear little herb, though regrettably untidy. It is useful for making a fresh, clean herb tea for drinking in hot weather, for using, fresh or dried, in cooking, and for bringing bees into the garden. It can be used as a border edging providing it is clearly established who is boss.

Lettuce

It's no use pretending it's easy — lettuce can be a tricky thing to grow. It has a root system which wants what it wants when it wants it or can turn cantankerous. It requires a steady supply of both moisture and nutriment and, if allowed to wilt when half-grown, will run to seed. You have to keep your eye on lettuce.

It enjoys the company of carrots, onions, strawberries and beetroot. Providing water requirements are observed a plot sown with lettuce, cabbage and beet will be relatively trouble-free.

When planted in alternate rows with radish it can thrive and, at the same time, protect the radish against the flea beetle.

Wood-ash scattered between the rows will help to protect it against insect depredations but, best of all, it appreciates the company of the French marigold or the African marigold — the Tagetes species. These small and showy plants should never be confined to the flower garden as they are front-line battlers against insects who hate the scent of their foliage and blossoms. Lettuce and French marigolds make as natural a marriage as ham and eggs.

Lily of the valley

The scent of the lily of the valley is such a delicious harbinger of spring that many people try to grow it and many fail because it does not have the hard winter conditions it needs. If you can offer a cold winter, semi-shade, a soil rich in humus and woodland conditions, plant out the 'pips' in early winter and top-dress with leaf-mould or peat. It will flower with the narcissus but don't ever put the cut flowers together in a vase because they can't abide each other and both of them will wilt.

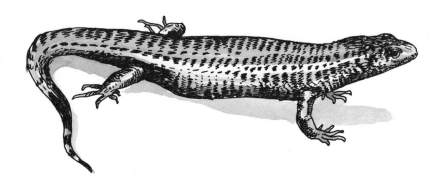

lizards patrol the garden and keep down snails, grasshoppers and beetles

Lizards

Happy the garden with lizards in it. Some of them look fierce but are not. If your dog's hackles rise when confronted with one, take him away and let the lizard escape. Lizards patrol the garden and keep down snails, grasshoppers and beetles. They climb trees in pursuit of the Christmas beetle. Even if they did no good at all the sight of a lizard on the path, soaking up the sun is reward enough.

lettuce enjoys the company of carrots, strawberries and beetroot

M
Mangoes

It sounds cruel but garden lore says it ensures a bumper crop of fruit. Starting at the bottom of the trunk of the tree hammer in a galvanised iron nail at about 1m intervals and continue until the branches start to spread.

Marigolds

I asked a friend what he understood by the term 'companion planting'.

'Marigolds with everything,' he said.

I grew up with marigolds. My grandmother used to scatter the dried petals on her soups and lived with calendula ointment and tincture at the ready for our grazes and wounds. Her garden burned with their colour. Orange is a colour many people love for its vitality and as many hate for its stridency. Fortunately the family, Compositae, is a large one and can offer flowers of soft cream, lemon and apricot too. But all of them have a strong and unpleasant odour. The strongest reek belongs to the smaller varieties, the French and African marigolds of the 'Tagetes' variety.

The roots of marigolds give off a substance which drives away the eel-worm. They are therefore good to plant near potatoes, tomatoes and roses.

Dogs won't cock their legs against pots which contain marigolds.

The Mexican beetle forsakes bean rows which have marigolds growing among them.

marigolds with everything

A clump is useful in every flower-bed; an edging gives protection for the veggies. One of the pleasantest I have seen is a border of French marigolds backed by the soft blue of ageratum which cooled their colour and gave charm.

Marigolds make good cut-flowers and are not difficult to grow. Their influence in a garden is all for good. You can indulge your colour preferences and still have 'marigolds with everything' and do a good job of 'companion planting'.

marjoram has good effects on plants growing near it

Marjoram

There are two varieties of marjoram, the 'sweet', which is an annual, and the 'pot' which is a perennial. You can't go wrong with either of them as both have a good effect on any plants growing near them and act as a repellent to insects. This is a medicinal herb which contains a volatile oil which, when distilled, can be used as a liniment.

Mealy bugs

Mealy bugs suck the life out of plants, but fortunately are one of the favourite foods of ladybirds. A spray with soapy water and a scrape-off with a knife is recommended by many experts but a brush soaked in methylated spirits applied direct to the pests, though a tedious exercise is not only satisfying but highly effective.

Mice

Mice are fond of pea and bean seeds. If you roll the seeds in paraffin before planting they will leave them alone.

Mignonette

This old-fashioned plant with its strange green and brown flowers has a fragrance of subtle delight. Grown as a low ground-cover for rose-beds it will benefit the bushes. Oddly, mignonette put in a vase with other flowers will kill them.

Mildew

Many plants such as begonias, are subject to mildew. Dried sage sprinkled around them will help, as will spraying with teas made from horsetail or nettle.

Millipedes

They may not look attractive but they do no harm. They live on decaying matter and do a clean-up job.

Mint

Mint is a 'must' for every garden. The bought mint-sauce is a pale shadow of the freshly-made.

Mint grows better in some shade. Planted near the house it will keep mice out; planted near the cabbage patch it will repel the cabbage white butterfly. Caterpillars and the flea beetle don't like it either.

Fresh or dried mint in the pantry will keep ants away; sachets of dried mint smell nice in the wardrobe and will repel the clothes moth.

Never plant mint near parsley. They don't like each other.

Monoculture

The planting of a mass of one species is a mistake. It's like lining up the silver in one place to make it easy for the burglar. Mixed plantings make for mutual protection. Plants which keep their roots near the surface should be the companions of those which root deeply. Two varieties of plant which both need moisture should not be planted together to fight for what is available. Monoculture is the most prevalent mistake made by gardeners. Nothing attracts pests more than the prospect of rich and easy feeding and, once ensconced, they multiply like mad.

Mosquitos

Mosquitos can be kept out of the house by pots of tansy or southernwood placed on windowsills and near outside doors.

Moths

The cabbage moth is kept away by dill planted in the vicinity and the clothes moth by mint or lavender sachets in the wardrobe and drawers.

Mulberries

Birds love mulberries and there are always enough on a tree to spare some. Once attracted to the garden birds do good work by eating all manner of insects although other fruit may need protection against them.

The mulberry is good for vines which grow happily near them and use them as a means to climb and spread.

Mulches

There are many gardeners who swear that the no-work garden is achieved by mulching. Mulches are fine, as far as they go. A mulch on poor soil is going to take a devil of a time to bring it up to scratch so, before applying a mulch of chopped leaves, or hay, or straw, it is as well to do your best for the soil underneath by giving it compost. Mulches keep down weeds and, when decomposed, add life to the soil but aesthetics enter into gardening and many people do not enjoy seeing their plants growing above anything but brown soil or green ground cover. I believe in mulches but like them concealed by soil — there is nothing pleasing about the sight of chopped newspaper or spiky hay between rows of growing plants for me. Leaves used as mulch should be shredded to give a porous blanket through which seedlings may push.

N

Nasturtiums

Nasturtiums are irritatingly rampant growers but, before you succumb to the impulse to rip them out, consider the good they do.

Orange-coloured nasturtiums repel aphids. If you leave them to grow under, and even to twine up, apple trees, they will control the spread of the woolly aphid.

Nasturtiums grown in the greenhouse will protect more precious plants against white-fly.

Nasturtiums secrete a mustard oil which insects find attractive and they will seek them out in preference to any cabbage, cauliflower, broccoli, Brussels sprouts, kohlrabi and turnips growing nearby. It therefore makes good sense to let them wander between these crops to act, not only as ground-cover to keep the soil moist, but as a decoy for insects and as a flavour-improving agent for your crops.

They are particularly good for giving radish a good hot taste, and for keeping away cucumber beetles.

Nettles

Nettles are weeds. The tidy gardener will make haste to get rid of them; but the nettle is a plant too rich in iron and nitrogen to be destroyed. It excretes silica, formic acid, nitrogen, iron and protein and so gives strength and flavour to any crop growing nearby. It also protects them against aphids, black fly and mildew.

If you find it growing in the potato patch or near your horse-radish plants, be grateful. It is particularly good for them both.

A tea made from nettles, as described under 'Herb teas' is useful both as a spray against aphids and to act as a tonic for your plants. The slush left should be added to the compost where it will help it to decompose more readily.

Another way of using nettles is to leave them in rainwater for three weeks and let them ferment. The liquid makes a good fertiliser.

Any lonely nettle found growing should be transplanted to the tomato area. The more nettles growing there the better chance for the tomatoes to escape mould.

If you just have to pull out nettles, don't burn them. If you have a compost bin, throw them in there; if you haven't chop them up and dig them into the soil where they can do nothing but good.

Newspaper

Newspaper is made from wood-pulp and is degradable. It can be shredded and added to the compost-bin or used directly on the soil. Overlapping thicknesses of newspaper, well-soaked, can go into the bottom of trenches. can be used as a layer below mulches of leaves to keep down weeds. Newspaper once lived and can go back to the soil from which it grew.

Nepeta

If you have cats it's nice to have cat-mint for the pleasure of seeing the ecstatic way they roll in it. If you don't have cats you can still grow nepeta as a deterrent against ants.

nasturtiums — consider the good they do

O
Onions

Onions can suffer badly from attack by thrips and it's unlikely that you'll have enough hover-flies around to protect your crop so make it part of a mixed planting. Onions grow well in alternate rows with carrots, which protect them against the onion-fly, and with beetroot, silver-beet and lettuce. A scattering of wood-ash between the rows will give them added protection.

Onions planted near apple-trees will ward off apple-scab and minced onion peelings dug into the rose-bed will help to keep the roses free of bugs.

A spray made by chopping up onions, with their skins to a milky consistency in the food-blender and diluting the resultant liquid by half, is useful against red spider and aphids, particularly the rose aphid.

Oregano

Some people call it o-*regg*-anno, others call it oreg-*ar*-no and it's a herb which can be used instead of marjoram which is the milder member of the family. Beetles and the white cabbage butterfly won't come near it so it's good to grow among the cabbages. A sprig or two of it on pantry shelves will keep pests away.

parsley and chives make good companions

P
Parsley

I get sick of hearing 'I can see who's boss *here!*' when our flourishing parsley is noticed. It is said to only grow well in a garden where the woman is the boss when actually it grows well when anyone has the sense to give it some shade and keep it away from mint. A few plants are never enough. A thick border is a joy. It takes a lot of parsley to keep up with family demand for use in cooking, as garnish, as a tea, to use as an astringent for the complexion and a conditioner for the hair.

Bees love it if you allow it to flower. Aphids don't, so it's good to grow near tomatoes, asparagus and roses. It is said to improve the taste of the fruit and the veggies and to increase the scent of the roses. Parsley and chives make good companions.

Parsnips

Parsnip dislikes are easy to remember. Carrot, celery, caraway.
They like peas, potatoes and pepper and won't fall out with beans,
radish or garlic.

Peach

The eternal vigilance needed to protect stone-fruits can put one off
trying to grow them. Tansy and garlic make a good first line of
defence.

Tansy is one of the best insect repellents. In the days when straw
and bracken were used to soften bare floors, tansy was added as a
'strewing herb' to help keep bugs at bay. You have only to see how
flying insects make a careful detour to avoid the growing plant to
realise how strongly their pungent scent is disliked. The peach-tip
moth and the fruit-fly are no exceptions.

Moth-balls hung among the branches are a protection against
curly-leaf, and, if you are unlucky enough to get it try spraying with a
mixture of nettle and horse-tail tea, or one of them if you don't have
access to both. If you can make enough to soak the soil around the
trees too, so much the better.

Pears

Grass roots give off an excretion which stops pear-tree roots from
growing so it's better to have an area of bald ground around the tree.

Peas

Peas grow well with most vegetables but heartily dislike being near
onions, shallots and garlic.

They should not be grown in the same place two years in
succession because they will have robbed the ground of the feed they
require.

Two rows of peas to one of potatoes is recommended as being of
benefit to both vegetables.

Low-growing plants such as radish, carrot and turnip are good to
grow with peas but make sure the carrots have the sunny side of the
rows.

Tall plants like the bean and sweet corn, and spreading plants like
cucumber do no harm to peas but it is as well to provide sufficient
room for them all to grow without too much encroachment on each
other.

Wood-ash sprinkled between the rows will protect peas.

parsnips like peas, potatoes and beans

Pennyroyal

This is a good herb to grow where ants are troublesome and to rub on the skin to keep mosquitos away.

Pepper

Pepper, shaken around plants, will protect them both against animals and some insects. Sprinkled on dew-wet leaves it will keep caterpillars away.

Potatoes

Potatoes grow well with peas, beans, cabbage and sweet corn.

Potatoes do not grow well near apple trees, cherry trees, cucumbers, pumpkin, sunflowers, tomatoes and raspberry canes, all of which make them susceptible to blight. I haven't heard whether the same goes for loganberries or the cultivated blackberry but since they are such close relations to the raspberry it might be as well not to take the chance with them either.

Potatoes and sunflowers stunt each other's growth — a fairly obvious situation, since both are strong growing plants and will compete with each other for nutriment.

Potatoes should be kept away from tomatoes. Exudation from their roots will stop the tomatoes growing well.

Broad beans and potatoes are good to grow together, two rows of beans to one of potatoes.

Green beans grown in alternate rows with potatoes will help to keep the Colorado beetle away.

If there is any chance of the Colorado beetle you can lure them away from your potatoes by planting egg-plant near-by. Even if you don't like egg-plant it is useful as a lure because beetles prefer it to the potato and will congregate on the plants and make themselves available for easy murdering.

Marigolds are said to repel both Colorado beetle and eel-worm.

Nasturtiums allowed to wander among the potato plants, a few horse-radish plants, and nettles left to grow, are all protection for the potato crop.

What exactly the pumpkin and the potato have against each other is not clear but their animosity is strong and mutual.

The potato beetle loves bran. A goodly supply sprinkled between the rows will offer an alternative food supply.

Praying mantis

The mantis is not an attractive insect. It looks what it is — a killer. It is one of the most ferocious creatures on earth and attacks anything moving. It seizes its prey between its forelegs and rips it apart with its

pepper protects plants from animals and some insects

powerful jaws. Beetles, spiders, aphids, caterpillars, leaf-hoppers, bugs, your finger if you are unwary enough to tease it, and other mantis, can all fall victim. It doesn't just kill pests which afflict the garden but the beneficent insects too, but, for all that, it can be useful so it may be as well to subdue the instinct to kill it on sight. You may have seen a brown lumpy mass as big as an egg attached to a leaf or twig. These are eggs laid by the female and are waiting for the spring, when they will hatch.

Primulas

If you want your primulas to be safe from the annoying attentions of birds which peck them, just plant them near the lavender hedge.

pumpkin

Pumpkins

(see also 'Squash')

Pumpkins and sweet corn grow well together as the pumpkin provides ground cover and is particularly effective during a hot, dry summer when it keeps the soil cool and conserves water for which the corn will be grateful. Pumpkins do not grow well near potatoes.

Pyrethrum

Pyrethrum is a pretty little plant which looks nice anywhere but is of particular value near strawberries to keep pests away.

Flies do not like its scent so it makes a good back-door plant.

The dust made from it is one of the insecticides which can be safely used except for the fact that it kills bees. If you use it in the evenings when the bees have retired for the night you need have no worries.

Q
Quassia

A spray made from quassia chips is good against caterpillars and aphids and can be used in the comfortable knowledge that it won't kill the ladybirds which live on the aphids. You can buy the chips at some health-food shops.

quassia chip spray does not harm helpful ladybirds
but will kill caterpillars

Put one tablespoon of chips in a litre of water, bring to the boil and then leave on a low simmer for two hours. The liquid should then be diluted with five times the amount of water for use against aphids and with four times the amount of water if you are up against caterpillars.

R

Radishes

Radishes grow well with lettuce which controls the flea beetle which attacks the radish.

They grow well near peas and the herb, chervil.

They grow badly near the herb hyssop.

Nasturtiums, which secrete a mustard-oil, give radish a sharper flavour if grown nearby.

Raspberries

Raspberries and blackberries do not grow well together.

Raspberries grown near potatoes make the potatoes more susceptible to blight.

Red spider (Two-spotted mite)

The red spider is now known as the two-spotted mite. They are so tiny that even an infestation is hard to spot with the naked eye, and they love dry and dusty conditions. They work on the underside of leaves, sucking the sap, and their presence is betrayed by a mottling, stippling and silvering of the leaf. A soap and water spray, with particular attention paid to the underside of all the leaves, will help. Better still, keep the two-spotted mite at bay by misting your plants in dry weather.

Rhubarb

If your rhubarb starts flowering there's something wrong. The plants are either short of water or food.

roses

Keep the weed, dock, away from your rhubarb plant as it encourages the presence of the yellow rhubarb beetle.

Short sticks of rhubarb dug in around the cabbages will help to protect them against club-root.

The leaves of rhubarb are strong in oxalic acid and while they may be good for cleaning aluminium they are poisonous to the stomach and should not be eaten, but they can be used to make a spray to use against aphids. A good solid chopped mass of them simmered in water to cover for half an hour and the liquid diluted to about a third strength makes a good spray to use at once but not to keep in store.

Never cook rhubarb in an aluminium saucepan — it's dangerous.

Robberfly

This ugly ferocious fly catches other insects on the wing and squirts them with its saliva to immobilise them before sucking out their body juices. It obviously must do some good for the gardener but it's up to you how you treat it.

Rosemary

The name comes from the Latin *ros marinus* — which means 'dew of the sea' and for the life of me I can't see how this shrubby, aromatic plant earned it. Certainly it grows well near the sea but it is also found in the Sahara Desert.

The active principle in rosemary is its aromatic volatile oil. Its use ranges from culinary to medical to beauty care. In the garden it earns its way by repelling mosquitos, and being a friendly companion to sage, both stimulating the herb's growth and strengthening its taste.

Rosemary and potatoes do not grow well near each other.

If you are making a separate herb garden a rosemary hedge kept well-trimmed, makes a good border. It also makes a protective edging to the cabbage plot for cabbage worm butterflies don't like it.

Roses

The aphid is the bane of the rose-grower. When planting a new rose bush put a clove of garlic to grow with it. The roots of the rose will take up the exudation from the garlic and so become less attractive to the greenfly.

Parsley grown with roses will also help against the pest.

Instead of throwing away your banana skins tuck them in the soil around your rose bushes and they will provide silica, calcium, sulphur phosphate and sodium on which the roses will thrive.

It's unlikely that you'll want to plant onions among your roses; garlic looks right in a way that onions do not, but onion skins can be chopped and dug into the soil. Both garlic and onions make roses smell all the sweeter.

Mignonette looks pleasant grown as a ground cover beneath rose bushes and the roses appreciate its presence.

A wide piece of plastic piping sunk about 30 centimetres deep into the ground by the side of a rose bush makes a good funnel for ensuring that water provided gets to the roots where it is needed and is not just dissipated a few inches below ground.

Rue

Rue is a dainty plant with feathery leaves and golden flowers. No insects will go near it. Slugs give it a wide berth. This 'herb of grace' was once used in exorcism by the Roman Catholic church. It grows easily from seed, enjoys full sun and is useful as an edging hedge, less than a metre high. Keep it away from sage and basil. It poisons both of them.

It is a good plant to have growing near doors and windows. Grown in a window-box it will keep flies out of the kitchen and a few plants near the barbecue area will keep them away from food.

rosemary

sage

S
Sage

Sage takes its name from the Latin *salvare* which means 'to heal' and owes its spread around Europe to the Romans who occupied so much territory. It is one of the most popular herbs, both for its culinary use and for its attractive appearance. The blue-grey leaves and blue flowers blend well with other plants provided it is not allowed to straggle.

Sage protects carrots against the carrot-fly and cabbages against the cabbage-moth. Cabbages are more tender when grown near sage.

Dried sage sprinkled around plants will protect them from lice and mildew.

Rue kills sage. Sprinkled, dry, in the wardrobe, sage kills moths.

Salt

If red spider mites and cabbage worms are extra troublesome a hot salt spray will get rid of them and, surprisingly, won't harm the plants. This is what I've heard but never had the nerve to try. A heaped tablespoon of salt dissolved in 4.5 litres of hot water is the strength recommended but it would be as well to soak the ground well afterwards to disperse the salt which could damage young and tender roots.

You can kill snails and slugs by putting salt on them but there are other, less messy methods.

Santolina

This is another plant which, when dried, can be used in clothes cupboards to keep away the moth. Roses like santolina. The shrub grows to about 60 centimetres high and if the silver-grey foliage is kept trimmed it can make a nicely domed little bush. Left untrimmed it becomes covered by a mass of yellow button flowers which light up the border.

Savory

Winter Savory is a perennial; Summer Savory is an annual. It is useful, planted between rows of beans where its peppery leaves inhibit the bean beetle. Onions appreciate it too.

Scale

A strong spraying with soapy water is an initial method of attack against scale. Always use soap and not detergent. (See 'soap'.) Rinse with clear water after spraying and be prepared to repeat the process fairly often.

Scorpion

There are scorpions and pseudo-scorpions so give anything you are doubtful about a wide berth as you could get a painful sting from the scorpion's tail. Both are worth leaving unmolested for the true scorpion eats cockroaches and the pseudo-scorpion, which does not sting, eats a variety of other insects.

Seaweed

Seaweed makes a marvellous fertiliser and can be used to make a spray. If you collect any from the beach wash it well when you get it home and add it to the compost bin, not as one great blanket, but in judicious thinnish layers. Seaweed is a good source of potash.

To make a spray, boil about 500 grams seaweed in 20 litres of water (you can, of course, make proportionally less) for an hour or until a lesser amount thickens. When the spray dries on the plant or tree it will have smothered the eggs and larvae of insects which will then come off with it.

Silver beet

Onions and beetroot are its favourite companions; it is also said to grow well near lavender.

Skinks

If you come across a little lizard with small flat scales hiding under a stone or in your flower-pots, welcome it. Skinks live among leaf litter and sprawling vegetation and eat snails, beetles and unwary moths.

Slugs

Slugs like even ground over which to travel and have difficulty negotiating crumbly compost or a covering of bark. They betray their presence by their slimy trails which they leave behind on their night-prowls. They don't like freshly-limed ground or wood-ash or the bitterness left behind on the soil by a watering with wormwood tea (see Herbal Teas). When confronted by a slug you can kill it by sprinkling salt over it. A kinder death can be offered by putting down saucers of beer for them to enjoy before drowning in an alcoholic daze.

Surprisingly there is a 'good' slug — the pestacella. It is pale yellow and has a small flat shell at its tail end. It feeds on other slugs and ground insects.

Snails

A morning tour of the garden after a wet night can make the hand-picking of snails a satisfactory but lengthy job. Cabbage leaves left on the ground at night will offer them cover from which they can be collected and destroyed. Birds encouraged to the garden, will help to keep the population down but not low enough. Hand to hand combat is the most effective way of getting rid of them, and citrus skins, left inverted among plants, will collect the pests in satisfying numbers for slaughter.

Soap

A soapy spray is made by dissolving 225 grams common laundry soap (not liquid detergent) in nine litres of water. After spraying, hose the plants down with clean water and repeat the two processes as often as seems necessary.

silverbeet

Southernwood

'Lad's love' or 'Old Man' has been used down the centuries for worms in children, female menstrual difficulties, baldness in men and moths in carpets. Its silver-grey leaves are bitter to the taste and have a sharp scent.

A hedge of southernwood will grow to less than a metre high and, if kept trimmed will look decorative while repelling the fruit-fly and the mosquito.

Spiders

There are over a thousand species of spider in Australia and only about 25 of them are dangerous to man. Chief among these is the funnel-web which should be killed on sight and gloves always worn when gardening where there is any likelihood of its presence.

Spiders live on insects and are useful in the garden. The St. Andrew's spider, so-called because of the cross on its back, stays immobile at the centre of its web during the day and hunts at night. The wolf spider hunts among garden litter and the bark spider under loose bark. All are valuable predators of insects which are a nuisance to the gardener.

Spinach

Spinach needs cool conditions and may run to seed in hot weather. It likes to grow near strawberries. Although it is rich in iron, calcium, and vitamins A and C it is also high in oxalic acid, so don't be like Popeye and live on it. Enjoy it served with lemon and butter or pureed with a sprinkling of nutmeg, fairly often but not frequently.

Squash

The term is here used for zucchinis, marrows, pumpkins, chokos, cucumber and melons, though you may call them cucurbits. They are all gross feeders and slugs just love them. Don't leave their pollination to the bees and other insects, take a personal hand. The female flower, unlike the male has a swelling behind the flower. You can use a cotton-bud or fine paint-brush to transfer the pollen from the male to the female flower, but, if they are close enough together, you can jam the open flowers together and give them a shake to transfer the pollen.

All squash are tastiest when small as when they become large they are mostly water and so tasteless.

An unusual variety to try is 'Vegetable Spaghetti'. The bright yellow fruits are about 20 centimetres in length and when boiled the flesh is very like spaghetti but has the advantage of being non-fattening.

strawberries

Strawberries

Strawberries dislike being near cabbage, cauliflower, Brussels sprouts, broccoli and gladioli. They need a well-drained soil and regular feeding and watering.

Strawberries enjoy growing near borage, lettuce, spinach and sage.

A mulch of crushed pine needles or fir-cones will give the fruit added flavour. A mulch of any sort will keep weeds down and prevent moisture loss. Try grass clippings, compost, sawdust, leaf mould or wood shavings.

An edging of pyrethrum round the strawberry bed will keep many pests away.

A low cage of wire-mesh over the bed will protect the fruit from the birds.

Sunflowers

The sunflower makes a spectacular display and attracts bees to the garden.

Squash and cucumber grow well in the shade of the tall plants.

Sunflowers should be kept well away from potatoes as they stunt each other's growth.

Sweet corn

Sweet corn is good when grown near broad beans, potatoes, melons, cucumber, squashes and these plants do well too.

Sweet corn, grown near tomatoes, will lure away the pest helicoverpa from them.

Sweet corn takes a lot of nitrogen from the soil and so it is good to have peas and beans as a following crop to replace it.

pumpkins and sweet corn grow well together

T

Tachinid flies

If you see a fly which doesn't look *quite* like an ordinary fly it is probably the tachinid, which eats cut-worms and caterpillars so can be spared.

Tansy

You may know tansy as 'Bachelor's buttons', a name which well describes the little yellow flowers which grow in a cluster at the top of the stems. With its pleasant, feathery leaves and bright colour it is one of the most cheerful and useful plants in the garden.

Tansy has a bitter taste and a strong odour. It makes a good insect repellent. I rub the crushed leaves on our dog's coat — it keeps away the fleas.

The leaves were used to make 'tea' and to flavour cakes, apple dishes and fruit puddings. They were also used medicinally but are no longer recommended.

Tansy is good to plant near cabbages, roses, raspberries and grapes, to name but a few of the plants it helps. It concentrates potassium in the soil and so benefits near-by growth.

Plant it wherever you need protection against cut-worms, cabbage-worms, ants, flies, mosquitos and fruit moth. It is particularly good beneath peach trees which it helps to stay healthy and, in addition, wards off flying insects and keeps borers away.

Tansy was one of the 'strewing herbs' used in the old days when it kept away bugs underfoot; today it can be used in the food cupboard to discourage ants and in the clothes cupboard to drive out moths or, better still, to prevent them settling in at all.

Chopped-up tansy makes a good activator for the compost-heap.

Tea leaves

Tea leaves are appreciated by both camellias and geraniums — in the soil round them, not over them of course. Also good for citrus fruit trees.

Thrips

Thrips are very small but can make a terrible mess of the leaves of bushes and flowers, eating away the green and leaving silvery disfiguring marks. They are less likely to attack plants growing near to pyrethrum.

all plants growing near thyme are invigorated by it

Thyme

There are many varieties of thyme — lemon, carroway, turkey, variegated, etc. and all are pleasant to have in the garden if only for the fact that they attract bees.

Thyme growing near plants of the cabbage family will keep the cabbage-root fly away. Dried thyme sprinkled around the rows will help too.

All plants growing near thyme are invigorated by it.

Thyme makes a pleasant small shrub or can be grown in pots as a salad herb for use in salads and to flavour tomatoes. The dried leaves are useful in cooking.

Thyme contains 'thymol', a powerful disinfectant and was used in incense burners to purify sick-rooms. Its oil is said to be more than ten times stronger than carbolic acid as a disinfectant.

Toads

Toads are very useful in the garden as they come out under cover of night and hunt slugs, cut-worms and many other insects. Unfortunately they also eat earthworms but nobody's perfect.

Tomatoes

Tomatoes grow well near asparagus, celery, parsley, basil, carrots and chives.

Tomatoes do not enjoy the company of rosemary, potatoes, kohlrabi and fennel.

Some people say keep tomatoes away from all members of the cabbage family; others say grow them together because tomatoes ward off the cabbage white butterfly. Since there seems doubt it seems better to me to rely on thyme, mint, hyssop, rosemary, southernwood and sage to look after the cabbage family and keep tomatoes away in case they should suffer from being gallant.

Tomatoes can be protected against the cut-worm by sowing iron nails in the soil around them; from nematodes by growing French marigolds nearby, and from mould by giving them the company of nettles.

If attacked by viruses, spray with milk.

Tomatoes grown near gooseberry bushes protect them against insect attack.

Tomatoes grown near apricot trees will harm them by a substance given off by their roots.

Tomato leaves contain a substance said to be more active than nicotine. A spray made from the water in which a handful of leaves have been soaking for a day can be used against aphids on fruit trees and rose bushes, and also against caterpillars.

Turnips

Turnips grow well with peas and appreciate the protection of wood ash sprinkled around them.

Farmers say 'if all else fails, grow turnips'. They are light feeders and nicest if harvested before they are fully mature.

tomatoes and basil — the perfect pair

Traps

Broad leaves or pieces of cardboard daubed with molasses or black treacle and put down at night will attract pests which can be disposed of in the morning.

Leave pieces of raw potato and carrot where you want to trap wire worms.

Leave a bucket of water under an outside light to attract and drown flying insects.

Orange or grapefruit cups left upside-down, lettuce and spinach leaves, will all attract night-feeders who will be found there sleeping the next day.

Shallow little containers of sugar-water, honey, beer, dried yeast, etc. will trap many pests while you sleep.

V
Vines

See 'Grapevines'.

Virus

Milk, whole or skimmed, makes a good spray to use when a plant shows signs of virus disease. If using dried milk, dissolve about 500 grams in 4½ litres of water.

W
Wallflowers

Wallflowers are good companions for apple trees. These fragrant perennials are best treated as annuals in a mild climate. They like full sun and a soil previously dressed with lime and old manure. To keep them alive for a long time as cut flowers, split the ends of the stem and crush lightly, dip into boiling water for a few seconds and then let them rest in deep water for half an hour.

Wasps

It's better to avoid a wasp than to kill it. Yellow jacket and paper wasps eat grubs, scale insects and caterpillars, and the braconid wasp injects her eggs into aphids, and the eggs and larvae of other insects and, when they hatch out, they eat up all the fatty tissue and the host dies. There are other intricate ways in which the wasp ensures its survival as a species and they all seem to be at the expense of insects.

Apart from exercising a useful control over pests, wasps, which are honey-feeders, help to pollinate the flower and fruit garden.

Water

A good hard jet of water will blast away aphids quite successfully. A dousing with hot water will help against other types of pest and is unlikely to hurt the plant. Not boiling water, of course.

Wood Ash

Wood ash between the rows is a protection against a variety of pests.

A light sprinkling around plants of cauliflower, onions, beetroot, turnip, peas and lettuce, will be beneficial.

Wormwood

Wormwood is one of the ingredients used in the making of Vermouth. It also keeps moths at a distance.

This is another aromatic plant with grey-green silvery leaves and small yellow flowers and should be kept to itself for its toxic root excretions that harm plants growing near it. Even other aromatic plants such as sage and fennel cannot cope with it.

But it is very useful to have in the vicinity of fruit trees as a guard against leaf-eating caterpillars, aphids, moths.

It discourages fleas and mosquitos, the cabbage-worm butterfly, slugs and mice. A tea of wormwood poured on the ground where you think slugs or mice are making a regular run will send them away.

If you are unfortunate enough to do yourself a damage while working in the garden and have been improvident enough to run out of disinfectant, a few leaves of wormwood left in boiling water for a short time and then allowed to cool enough to be used as a poultice on the wound, will tide you over.

After washing the dog a drenching of wormwood tea (see Herbal Teas) will help to get rid of its fleas.

wallflowers — good companions for apple trees

Y
Yarrow

Yarrow, once regarded as a weed, is now a garden favourite. It is a pleasant plant with feathery leaves and flower colours white, yellow, red and pink. There are dwarf plants and tall ones and all are useful for blending among other plants where they increase the vitality of their neighbours.

If you find your soil is deficient in copper you need yarrow as a fertiliser. It is valuable when added to the compost and also for making herb tea (see Herb Teas) which can be used as a liquid medicine. Yarrow tea is also said to be good for rheumatism, and the young leaves, when chewed, give temporary relief from toothache.

Z
Zucchini

What could look nicer than the bold colours of the nasturtium against the deep green of zucchini leaves? Apart from helping to create a pleasant picture, the nasturtiums will be protecting the zucchini against aphids.

Good Companions
Bad Companions
Guide

Good Companions

Apples	Chives, Horsetail (Equisetum), Foxgloves, Wallflowers, Nasturtiums, Garlic, Onions
Apricots	Basil, Tansy, Southernwood
Asparagus	Tomatoes, Parsley, Basil
Basil	Tomatoes, Asparagus, Parsley, Apricots
Beans	Carrots, Cucumbers, Cabbages, Lettuce, Peas, Parsley, Cauliflower, Spinach, Summer Savory
Beans, broad	Potatoes, Sweetcorn
Beans, Dwarf	Beetroot, Potatoes
Beetroot	Onions, Silverbeet, Kohlrabi, Lettuce, Cabbage, Dwarf Beans
Borage	Strawberries
Brussells Sprouts	Nasturtiums
Cabbages	Beans, Beetroot, Celery, Mint, Thyme, Sage, Onions, Rosemary, Dill, Potatoes, Chamomile, Oregano, Hyssop, Southernwood, Nasturtiums, Tansy, Coriander
Carrots	Peas, Radishes, Lettuce, Chives, Sage, Onions, Leeks
Cauliflowers	Celery, Beans, Tansy, Nasturtiums
Celery	Tomatoes, Dill, Beans, Leeks, Cabbage, Cauliflowers
Chamomile	Mint, Cabbages, Onions
Chervil	Dill, Coriander, Radish

Good Companions

Chives	Parsley, Apples, Carrots, Tomatoes
Citrus	Guava
Coriander	Dill, Chervil, Anise, Cabbages, Carrots
Cucumbers	Potatoes (early crop only), Beans, Celery, Lettuce, Sweet Corn, Savoy Cabbages, Sunflowers, Nasturtiums
Dill	Carrots, Tomatoes, Cabbage, Fennel, Coriander
Fennel	Dill, Coriander
Foxgloves	Tomatoes, Potatoes, Apples
Fuchsias	Basil, Gooseberries, Tomatoes
Horseradish	Fruit trees, Potatoes
Hyssop	Grapevines, Cabbages
Kohlrabi	Beetroot, Onions
Garlic	Roses, Apples, Peaches
Geraniums	Grapevines
Grapevines	Geraniums, Mulberries, Hyssop, Basil, Tansy
Guava	Citrus
Leeks	Carrots, Celery
Lettuce	Carrots, Onions, Strawberries, Beetroot, Cabbages, Radishes, Marigolds

Good Companions

Marigolds	Lettuce, Potatoes, Tomatoes, Roses, Beans
Melons	Sweet Corn
Mint	Cabbages, Chamomile
Nasturtiums	Apples, Cabbages, Cauliflowers, Broccoli, Brussels Sprouts, Kohlrabi, Turnips, Radishes, Cucumbers, Zucchini
Onions	Carrots, Beetroot, Silverbeet, Lettuce, Chamomile, Kohlrabi, Summer Savory
Oregano	Cabbages
Parsley	Tomatoes, Asparagus, Roses, Chives
Parsnips	Peas, Potatoes, Peppers, Beans, Radishes, Garlic
Peaches	Tansy, Garlic, Basil, Southernwood
Peas	Potatoes, Radishes, Carrots, Turnips
Potatoes	Peas, Beans, Cabbage, Sweetcorn, Broad Beans, Green Beans, Nasturtiums, Marigolds, Foxgloves, Horse Radish, Egg Plant
Pumpkins	Sweetcorn
Radishes	Lettuces, Peas, Chervil, Nasturtiums
Raspberries	Tansy
Roses	Garlic, Parsley, Onions, Mignonette, Marigolds

Good Companions

Sage	Carrots, Cabbages, Strawberries
Savory	Beans, Onions
Silverbeet	Onions, Beetroot, Lavender
Spinach	Strawberries
Squash	Sunflowers
Strawberries	Borage, Lettuce, Spinach, Sage, Pyrethrum
Sunflowers	Squash, Cucumber
Sweetcorn	Broad Beans, Potatoes, Melons, Tomatoes, Cucumber, Squash, Tansy
Tansy	Cabbage, Roses, Raspberries, Grapes, Peaches
Thyme	Cabbage family
Tomatoes	Asparagus, Celery, Parsley, Basil, Carrots, Chives, Marigolds, Foxgloves, Garlic, Sweetcorn
Turnips	Peas, Nasturtiums
Wallflowers	Apples
Zucchini	Nasturtiums

Bad Companions

Apples	Grass, Potatoes
Apricots	Tomatoes, Basil, Sage
Beans	Onions, Garlic, Fennel, Gladioli, Sunflowers, Kohlrabi
Beetroot	Tall beans
Broccoli	Strawberries
Cabbages	Rue, Strawberries, Tomatoes, Garlic
Carnations	Hyacinths
Cauliflowers	Strawberries
Coriander	Fennel
Fennel	Beans, Tomatoes, Kohlrabi, Coriander, Wormwood
Garlic	Peas, Beans, Cabbages, Strawberries
Gladioli	Strawberries, Beans, Peas
Hyacinth	Carnations
Hyssop	Radishes
Kohlrabi	Tomatoes, Beans, Fennel
Mint	Parsley
Parsley	Mint
Parsnip	Carrots, Celery, Caraway

Bad Companions

Pears	Grass
Peas	Onions, Shallots, Garlic, Gladioli
Potatoes	Apples, Cherries, Cucumbers (with any but early crops), Pumpkins, Sunflowers, Tomatoes, Raspberries, Rosemary
Pumpkins	Potatoes
Radishes	Hyssop
Raspberries	Blackberries, Potatoes
Rosemary	Potatoes
Rue	Sage, Basil
Sage	Basil, Rue, Wormwood
Strawberries	Cabbages, Cauliflowers, Brussels Sprouts, Gladioli, Tomatoes, Broccoli, Garlic
Sunflowers	Potatoes
Tomatoes	Rosemary, Potatoes, Kohlrabi, Fennel, Apricots, Strawberries, Dill
Wormwood	all other plants